MW00876533

How to Buy Your Perfect First Home

What Every First-Time Homebuyer Needs to Know

Disclaimer

This book is not intended to be a substitute for personalized advice from a real estate agent or attorney. Nothing contained within this text should be construed as legal advice. The publisher and author make no representation or warranty as to this book's adequacy or appropriateness for any purpose. Similarly, no representation or warranty is made as to the accuracy of the material in this book.

Purchasing this book does not create any client relationship or other advisory, fiduciary, or professional services relationship with the publisher or with the author. *You alone* bear the *sole* responsibility for assessing the merits and risks associated with any real estate, tax, or financials decisions you make.

How to Buy Your Perfect First Home

What Every First-Time Homebuyer Needs to Know

By Anthony S. Park

Copyright © 2018 Anthony S. Park
All rights reserved. No part of this publication may be
reproduced or distributed without the express permission
of the author.
ISBN: 9781731350121
www.anthonyspark.com

Cover photo by Brina Blum on Unsplash

Dedication

For my amazing family,
the starting point of any perfect home

Thank you for your feedback

Hearing directly from you, the reader, is the best way for me to make these books as useful as possible.

Please share how this book has helped you, or any suggestions for how I can make it better. You can email me at homebuyer@anthonyspark.com or call me at 212-401-2990.

I thank you in advance for your feedback.

Best,
Anthony S. Park

TABLE OF CONTENTS

INTRODUCTION

Buying a home may be the biggest purchase you'll ever make, and it can feel overwhelming. But it doesn't have to.

WHO IS THIS BOOK FOR?

This book is for first-time homebuyers, but also for folks who may be upgrading to their second home. Maybe you don't remember the ins and outs of your first home purchase. Or perhaps the first time did not go as smoothly as you would've liked. Whether you are a first-time or second-time buyer, this book is intended to help you understand and navigate the homebuying process from start to finish.

This book is also for buyers who are financially stable and ready for their first home purchase. It does **not** focus on things like credit repair, down payment assistance, or "no money down" homebuying.

Finally, this book is for folks who are looking for a home in the city or suburbs, not small towns or the rural countryside. Because I live and practice in New York City, and because the Big Apple is a unique market, I've included NYC-specific notes throughout the book.

WHY A HOMEBUYER'S GUIDE IS SO IMPORTANT

If you think about it, buying a home is actually <u>three</u> of your biggest financial decisions wrapped into one:

1. Your home is your biggest purchase
2. Your mortgage is your biggest loan
3. Your real estate broker is your biggest professional bill

If you make the right decisions, you'll only pay the best price and rates for your home, mortgage, and broker.

If you make the wrong decisions, you'll spend every day living in a reminder of those mistakes.

THE GOAL OF THIS BOOK

My goal is for this guide to be an easy-to-understand overview of the entire homebuying process, so that you won't feel in the dark for any of the many steps.

I assume your goal is to gain just enough knowledge to work with your real estate team intelligently (because you probably have better things to do than read hundreds of pages or dozens of blogs trying to become a real estate expert).

After you read this guide, I recommend that you work with a real estate agent or attorney to get personalized advice.

So why bother reading the guide at all?

1. You may realize that the process isn't as complicated as you feared, and
2. When you start to work with your real estate professionals, you'll have a basic level of understanding ahead of time.

A BRIEF OUTLINE

This book is broken down into three sections:

Chapters 1 through 4 cover **Getting Prepared**, including knowing your timeline, setting your budget, and understanding your mortgage.

Chapters 5 and 6 cover **Home Shopping**, including choosing the perfect neighborhood, knowing your deal breakers, and starting your home hunt.

And Chapters 7 through 9 discuss **Closing the Deal**, including choosing your team, negotiating your offer, and completing all of the steps to closing.

Let's get started.

CHAPTER 1.

THINKING OF BUYING A HOME? DO THESE 5 THINGS FIRST

Buying your first home is a big deal. It's probably the largest and most consequential purchase you'll ever make. And when you sign on the dotted line for your home loan, you're pledging a significant chunk of your income to the bank or mortgage company for the next 15 to 30 years. It's a huge commitment.

Buying a home isn't as simple as buying a car—there's far more to the process than simply choosing a place you like and applying for a loan. Go that route, and you'll likely pay tens or hundreds of thousands more for your home over the long haul than someone better prepared to buy.

A savvy first-time homebuyer starts the process months or even *years* in advance. Before you call up a real estate agent, take these steps so that you're prepared to make the best choice for your home purchase.

STEP 1: SAVE MONEY LIKE YOUR LIFE DEPENDS ON IT.

When people ask how much to save before buying a home, most of them know there's a down payment involved. But many aren't aware of the other costs that come with homeownership.

Let's start with the down payment. The down payment is calculated as a percentage of your home's purchase price. All lenders expect you to put *some* money down. Depending on the lender and type of loan, the down payment can vary from as little as 3.5% for Federal Housing Administration (FHA) loans to 20% or more with conventional loans to avoid fees and get the best rates.

New York Note: If you're looking at co-ops, you'll be asked to put down at least 10%, and perhaps as much as 50% at high-end buildings.

That's a *lot* of money, no matter how you look at it. And it's only the beginning. You'll also have closing costs (generally between 2% and 5% of the purchase price), moving expenses (which can be several thousand dollars), and costs for new furnishings and home decor. The banks know you'll have these extra expenses, so they expect to see money left in your account *after* your down payment is met.

And if you've never owned a home before...be prepared for endless big and little expenses for maintenance and repairs you never saw coming. As a rule of thumb, plan to spend about 1% of your home's purchase price (or $5,000 on a $500,000 home) each year to maintain it.

Buying an older home or a charming fixer-upper? You should set aside double or even triple that amount.

Renovations, repairs, and remodeling can cost thousands and thousands of dollars.

Cultivate an aggressive saving habit now so you have the money you need to get a favorable mortgage—and money in the bank to cover moving, furnishings, and repairs and maintenance your first year.

STEP 2: GET RID OF DEBT.

Paying down debt is one of the most important things to do before buying a home. Lenders use your debt-to-income (DTI) ratio to qualify you for a mortgage. In other words, a great income is only half the picture. If you have too much going out in debt payments each month, you won't qualify for the mortgage you want (or you may not get one at all).

You need a DTI of 43% at an absolute minimum to qualify for a mortgage with most lenders, but you'll have more options and get the best rates if you're at 36% or below.

Here's how it works: let's say your income is $150,000 per year, or $12,500 a month gross. At 36% DTI, your total monthly payments, including your proposed mortgage, taxes, homeowners insurance, and homeowners' association (HOA) or condo fees can't exceed $4,500. But let's say that you are also regularly paying down debt at $2,000 a month. Your available cash for housing then drops to just $2,500.

New York Note: If you're looking at co-ops or condos, the 36% to 43% DTI may not apply. Many buildings are notorious for setting their own income-to-debt limits, so check the specifics for any building you're interested in.

What if you have high debt and low savings? Most financial advisors encourage you to pay down your debt first to avoid paying high interest charges, and focus on building a six-month emergency savings fund before saving for a house. If you're in that situation right now, you may need to postpone your dream of homeownership for a year or two.

STEP 3: PRACTICE LIVING ON A "MORTGAGE BUDGET."

Now that you know what you might qualify for based on your income and debt, figure out what you'd like to spend on your mortgage each month and write up a budget using that figure. If you're currently paying $2,000 a month in rent and you're looking at a $3,000 mortgage payment, practice living without that extra $1,000 a month for a while.

Your budget might look great on paper, especially if you're living with a lot of disposable income. But it can be harder than you think to make lifestyle changes to accommodate a hefty increase in your housing payment. And remember, the extra $1,000 for a mortgage payment is only part of the actual difference between your current rent and future housing costs—you'll still need to save for maintenance, repairs, and potentially higher utility bills in your new home.

If you can live comfortably on your "mortgage budget" for three or four months, you're probably ready to think about homeownership. If you're miserable with the changes in your lifestyle, or you're continually going over budget, you may need to scale back on your housing expectations.

Remember: what *you* think you need to live comfortably, and what the *bank* thinks you can afford, may be two very different things. It's always better to go with what you *know* you can manage, even if the bank approves you for more.

STEP 4: CLEAN UP YOUR CREDIT REPORT.

Wondering what to check before buying a home? Start with your credit file. Even if you have good credit and you've never been turned down for a loan, it's still a good idea to go over your credit report before you apply for a mortgage so you know what rates you'll qualify for.

You can usually get a free copy of your credit report if you have a major credit card with financial institutions like Citibank or Capital One. If you don't have a major credit card, you can get a free credit report once a year from the three main credit bureaus at www.annualcreditreport.com. Look it over carefully for any errors or discrepancies, and contact the creditors to correct them.

Although lenders have different criteria, you generally need a FICO score of at least 620 to qualify for a conventional mortgage. Higher scores mean lower interest rates, which save you tens or even hundreds of thousands in interest payments over the life of your loan.

For example, with a FICO score of 760 or above, you might get a 30-year, fixed-rate mortgage at 4.25% interest. If you borrow $400,000, you'll pay about $308,000 in interest by the end of the loan.

If your score is 620, however, you might pay 6% for the same loan, which would end up costing you about $465,000 in interest. In addition, your monthly payment would be about $500 higher at 6% than at 4.25%. It's definitely in your best interest to clean up your credit report and build up the highest credit score possible before you apply for a mortgage.

Keep in mind that you have more than one credit score. Different credit reporting agencies and financial institutions often use different scoring models. Although the FICO score is the most widely known, most lenders have their own proprietary model, so your actual numbers may vary. However, an excellent FICO score usually translates to an excellent credit score with any of the other scoring models, so it's a good benchmark to help you know what interest rate you can expect.

STEP 5: RESEARCH YOUR LOCAL HOUSING MARKET.

If you're thinking about homeownership, you've probably done a little research already. You may have read through the real estate listings, walked a few neighborhoods, and even visited an open house or two to get a feel for what you like.

But researching the housing market is about more than just knowing what neighborhoods and home styles you prefer—it's about understanding the economic factors that affect home prices and determining the right time to buy.

Although you can get an overview of larger housing trends by watching the national market, real estate is ultimately an extremely local industry. The housing market functions quite differently in suburban areas than it does in Manhattan or the boroughs, so you need current data about the specific areas you're interested in.

Start with local multiple listing service (MLS) data. You can get quality information from sites such as Realtor.com without signing with an agent. Many title companies and local real estate brokers publish quarterly market reports providing a wealth of useful information about what's available, what's selling fast, and what to expect in the future. You can also get "Zestimates" from Zillow for homes you're interested in, and see real-time price trends on those properties.

New York Note: The site Streeteasy.com is currently one of the best places to get real-time market information on condos and co-ops in the five boroughs.

You'll want to know whether you're in a buyer's market or a seller's market. In a buyer's market, the inventory of available homes exceeds the number of buyers, and you're more likely to get a discounted price or other concessions. In a seller's market, there are more buyers than available homes, and you could find yourself in a bidding war for desirable properties. If market data suggest a seller's market, you might want to put off buying a home right now, unless you're happy settling for less house for your money.

ONE LAST THING...

Don't let misguided notions of homeownership as a rite of passage dictate your buying decision. Owning a home isn't always the best choice, from either a financial or personal satisfaction point of view. Renting is a great option, especially if you're unable or unwilling to commit to a home for the next 10 years or so.

On the other hand, if you're sure you're ready to buy a house, put in the work to do it right. You stand a much better chance of getting the right home at a great price—and the best terms on your mortgage.

KEY TAKEAWAYS:

- Start preparing for the homebuying process at least six months to a year in advance to get the best terms on a mortgage.
- You need a lot more in your savings account than just a down payment. Lenders expect to see a solid cushion of cash left over after closing.
- Excess debt, even if you pay on time, can prevent you from getting the mortgage you want.
- Recognize cycles in your local housing market so you don't pay more than you should for your home.

CHAPTER 2.

HOW LONG DOES THE HOMEBUYING PROCESS TAKE?

You already know that buying a house is unlike buying just about anything else. You can't just choose one out of a catalog, whip out your American Express, and sign a receipt. It's a long, occasionally arduous journey with more than a few potential pitfalls along the way.

Too many people approach homebuying without understanding how it actually works. They look for shortcuts, wondering how to speed up the process. The truth is, it can take a year or more to close on a house, depending on your financial situation and local housing market.

According to Trulia, the average homebuyer spends between four and six months preparing to shop for a home, between 60 and 90 days actively looking at properties, a week negotiating a contract, and between 30 and 60 days closing the deal. Of course, not every buyer is "average."

If you're wondering how early to start the homebuying process, the answer is: it depends on your finances and the market. If you've got a tidy sum in the bank, your credit is squeaky-clean, and you're in a buyer's market, you could close on a house in about three months.

On the other hand, if your savings are meager, your credit score needs work, or home inventory is low, it could take a year or more to buy a house.

Here's what you need to know about the homebuying timeline and what to expect every step of the way.

BEFORE YOU BUY

6 Months Plus: Pre-purchase prep

If you have a moving date in mind—perhaps your lease is expiring in a few months—you should start preparing to buy a house at least six months in advance.

Start with a deep dive into your finances:

- Figure out exactly how much money you have for a down payment. If you're using your personal savings, don't wipe it out. Be sure to leave a decent cushion for other expenses—you'll need it and your lender expects it. If you're counting on a relative to boost your down payment, find out what they're planning to give and ask them to write a letter confirming the money is a gift, even if you eventually plan to pay it back.
- Calculate your debt-to-income ratio (the sum of all your monthly loan and credit card payments divided by your gross monthly income). If the figure is higher than 36%, pay off a few accounts before you apply for a mortgage.

- Request your FICO score. If it's below 620, take steps to bring it up—you'll have trouble getting a conventional loan otherwise. To get the best loan terms, aim for a credit score of 720 or above. It's a good idea to review your credit report for errors and discrepancies. If you find one, it can take up to three months to remove it and update your credit score.

- Go over your budget and figure out a mortgage payment you think you can afford. Of course, your lender will ultimately decide what you qualify for, but it's a good idea to run a few numbers on your own. Don't forget to include expenses that aren't counted in your debt-to-income ratio such as utility bills, which may be higher in a new home.

You should also start gathering information about neighborhoods you're interested in. Drive around, or better yet, spend an afternoon exploring them on foot. Check property listings to see what homes are selling for, how long they sit on the market, and whether prices are trending up or down. Take a few virtual tours of homes for sale in neighborhoods you like, or visit a few open houses.

Make a list of must-haves for your new home. This list will save you (and your realtor) countless hours looking at homes you'll never want to buy. Try not to get too hung up on one particular feature, though—chances are good you'll have to compromise to find the right home at a favorable price.

2-3 Months: Assemble your team

Start your due diligence on realtors, lenders, and real estate attorneys. Ask everyone you know for recommendations and request phone interviews with promising candidates.

Go online and compare rates from different lenders. Read up on the application and approval process, and find out what fees are involved in processing a mortgage. Learn about the different types of mortgage products (fixed-rate versus adjustable, for example) and think about which one works best for you.

Keep in mind, most real estate brokers and agents have relationships with certain lenders and attorneys. It's fine to consider them, but you aren't obligated to use your realtor's preferred professionals.

1 Month: Get your paperwork in order

Get pre-approved for a mortgage with the lender of your choice. This signals to sellers that you're a serious buyer—and it gives you a price ceiling for homes you can afford. Most pre-approval letters are good for 90 days, so you have some time to shop.

You should also begin gathering the documents your lender will need for underwriting. You should have tax returns for you and any co-applicant for the past two years; checking, savings, and investment account statements for the most recent three to six months; and your last few pay stubs.

HOUSE HUNTING

1-3 Months: Zero in on a home

During this time, you'll be actively looking at homes on the market. You or your realtor should set up saved searches on MLS and other listing platforms so you're notified whenever a new listing turns up in an area you're interested in.

Don't limit yourself to homes at the top end of your price range—you may find a better fit and get more value for your money with lower-priced homes.

If inventory is low, your search may take longer than a couple of months. Don't give up—it's better to wait and keep looking than commit to something you won't be happy with a few months or years down the road.

If the search drags on, you may need to renew your pre-approval letter from your lender. Make sure you're adding current bank statements and pay stubs to your document collection.

1-2 Weeks: Negotiate a contract

Once you find a home you want to buy, write an offer with your realtor. The offer includes more than just the price you're willing to pay for the home. A purchase offer, which becomes a binding contract if the seller accepts, includes:

- The amount of earnest money you're putting down (earnest money is a deposit that demonstrates your intention to buy the home—it is held in escrow and applied to your down payment before you close on the house)

- Information about who will pay for title insurance, inspections, and buyer's closing costs
- How costs such as taxes will be prorated
- A target closing date
- Any contingencies such as financing and home inspection reports

The seller will probably submit a counteroffer, which you can accept or counter with a new offer of your own. Be sure you have a bottom-line number in mind before you begin negotiations, and don't be afraid to walk away if the counteroffer is too high.

Once you have an agreement signed by both parties, you enter the contract-to-close phase of the homebuying process.

CLOSING THE DEAL

30-60 Days: Contract to close

This is the homestretch of the homebuying process: you're almost there, but things can still derail closing.

Your lender begins the process by preparing a good-faith estimate of closing costs, principal and interest payments, and escrow payments for taxes and insurance. You'll lock in an interest rate, set a tentative closing date, and have your lender submit your loan package to underwriting for approval.

Your attorney represents your interests in the closing process. He handles your title report and works with your lender to get all your documents in order. Your attorney also prepares a settlement statement showing what you owe the seller and/or the seller's lender, the title company, and others at closing.

You have a lot of responsibilities during this period as well:

- Choose a homeowners insurance company and share that information with your lender
- Schedule a home inspection
- Give notice to your landlord
- Transfer the balance of your down payment to your escrow account and make sure your closing funds are easily accessible, including any gifts from relatives
- Arrange for movers, unless you're planning a DIY move, and begin packing nonessentials
- Contact utility companies to establish service in your name at your new address
- If your contract includes a final walk-through, schedule this for as close to the day before closing as possible

New York Note: If you're buying a condo or co-op, you'll also need to complete the board application package and win approval from the board. Co-ops generally require an in-person interview in addition to the written paperwork. You need to prepare carefully for this interview: co-op boards have the power to turn you down, even if your financing is squared away.

1 Day: Closing and loan funding

Ask your attorney for a checklist of things you need to bring to closing. At a minimum, you'll need your ID, the name and contact information for your mortgage broker or loan officer, and your checkbook, unless your attorney tells you to bring certified funds.

Verify the date, time, and closing location a day in advance. Be prepared to spend a couple of hours verifying and signing paperwork. Once all the documents are in order, the seller's representative will turn over the keys to your new home.

KEY TAKEAWAYS:

- It takes the average homebuyer about four and a half months to close on a house, although it can take up to a year or more in some cases.
- You can shorten the homebuying process with a mortgage pre-approval letter and well-organized financial documents.
- A signed contract doesn't always lead to closing—contingencies can and do derail the process.
- You need a team of reputable professionals to help you navigate the homebuying process.

CHAPTER 3.

HOW MUCH HOME CAN I AFFORD?

Buying more house than you can afford is a major mistake many first-time homebuyers make. And if you fall into that trap, your dream home can become a nightmare pretty quickly.

If you're looking for a quick answer, there are online calculators that show you how to set a homebuying budget. Although these tools are great for a rough estimate, you really need to understand your own finances and lifestyle before you settle on a budget.

Homeownership requires a lot more than making your monthly mortgage payment—there are property taxes, homeowners insurance, routine maintenance, and required repairs. And if you're like most new homeowners, you'll have lots of projects in mind to make the place your own.

Before you start shopping, here's what you need to know to set your homebuying budget.

HOW MUCH WILL THE BANK APPROVE FOR A HOME?

Most lenders follow the "28/36 rule" when it comes to home mortgages. This rule says you should spend no more than 28% of your gross monthly salary on housing, and no more than 36% of your salary on all debt, including your home, car, and other installment loans.

In other words, if you make $150,000 a year, your housing costs should be no more than about $3,500 a month—and your total monthly payments on all loans shouldn't exceed $4,500.

But remember, that $3,500 housing figure isn't just your mortgage principal and interest payment: it also includes property taxes and homeowners insurance. According to WalletHub, the median property tax bill in New York is about $4,400, which translates to just under $400 a month. Homeowners insurance averages $1,200 a year, or $100 a month.

Depending on where or what you buy, you may also have homeowners association fees, condo fees, or monthly maintenance fees that the bank includes in your 28% housing allowance.

Of that $3,500 housing figure, only $2,000 or $2,500 might go to principal and interest, while the rest goes to taxes, insurance, and fees.

> **New York Note**: If you buy a condo or co-op, monthly maintenance fees average about $1,500 a month.

There's another thing to keep in mind when you're working with bank ratios like the 28/36 rule: banks often approve you for more than you can comfortably afford. After all, the bigger your mortgage, the more they make.

It's better to take a more personal approach to setting your homebuying budget. Many personal finance experts recommend no more than 25% of your *take-home* pay for housing if you want to have enough cash to save responsibly and live comfortably in your new home.

Using the $150,000 salary example, your take-home pay would be in the neighborhood of $8,500 a month after taxes, 401(k) contributions, and health insurance or health savings account (HSA) deductions—dropping your housing budget to just over $2,100 a month.

Obviously, everyone's financial situation and lifestyle preferences are different, but it's always a good idea to work out how much *you* can comfortably spend—regardless of what *the bank* approves—to calculate how much house you can afford. No one likes to be house-poor.

HOW MUCH DOWN PAYMENT SHOULD YOU PAY?

Most lenders want 20% down on conventional loans, although there are lenders and loan programs that accept down payments of 10% or less. There's a catch, though: you'll pay primary mortgage insurance, or PMI, if you can't put down 20%.

PMI protects your lender in the event that you default on your mortgage. Depending on your credit score, the lender, and the amount of the loan, PMI usually costs between 0.5% and 1.0% of the loan amount *per year*.

In other words, if you take out a $500,000 mortgage, your PMI will be between $2,500 and $5,000 a year, or $200 to

$400 a month. You'll pay PMI every year until your loan balance drops below 80% of the value of your home.

If you don't have 20% for a down payment, you may qualify for an FHA loan with as little as 3.5% down. Although the government insures the loan, you still pay mortgage insurance. The going rate is 1.75% of the loan amount upfront and annual premiums of 0.45% to 1.05%.

Too many homebuyers want to know the lowest possible down payment they can make to get into a home, but a bigger down payment can actually make the most financial sense. Your monthly payments will be lower and you'll get the best interest rates. That can mean tens or hundreds of thousands of dollars in interest savings over the life of the loan.

Compare the costs of a $500,000 home at 10% down, 20% down, and 30% down:

Terms	Down Payment	Total Interest Paid	PMI (0.5%)	Monthly Payment*
30-year 5%	10% ($50,000)	$420,000	$14,500	~$3,000
30-year 4.75%	20% ($100,000)	$350,000	$0	~$2,500
30-year 4.25%	30% ($150,000)	$269,000	$0	~$2,100

*Principal, interest, estimated taxes, and insurance.

CAN THE DOWN PAYMENT FOR A MORTGAGE BE GIFTED?

If you need help to reach the 20% down payment for a conventional loan, you can get help from a friend or relative, but there are certain guidelines that apply.

As of 2018, if you're buying a primary residence and it's a single-family home, the entire down payment can be a gift. You don't need to chip in any of your own money.

If the home is your primary residence, but it's a multi-family home, you don't have to contribute to the down payment if you're putting down 20% or more. If your down payment is less than 20% of the purchase price, then at least 5% must come from your own funds.

The donor needs to write a gift letter for the underwriter certifying that the money is a gift and not a loan. The letter also needs to include the donor's relationship to you, the amount of the gift, the date the money was transferred, and the address of the home you're buying.

CAN THE DOWN PAYMENT BE BORROWED?

Back in the bad old days of the housing crisis, lenders would make two piggyback "80-20" mortgages to help borrowers get into a new home with next to nothing down. The first mortgage was a conventional mortgage at 80% of the home value, and the second covered the 20% "down payment." These 80-20 loans had a high default rate, and fortunately, they're pretty much a thing of the past.

Today's combination loans are more likely to be 80-10-10 loans: an 80% conventional mortgage, a 10% home equity line of credit (HELOC) to boost the down payment, and 10% customer cash down. Some buyers go this route to avoid PMI and get better terms on their mortgage. Others use it to avoid the stricter lending requirements on a jumbo loan.

If you're considering borrowing 10% to avoid PMI, be sure to do the calculations so you know you're really coming out ahead. You may get a marginally better interest rate on an 80% mortgage versus a 90% mortgage, but the interest payments on the 10% HELOC can wipe out those savings, as well as the savings from PMI premiums.

USING A 401(K) ACCOUNT FOR A DOWN PAYMENT ON A HOUSE

In a word: don't.

Although IRS rules allow you to borrow up to 50% of your account balance, or $50,000, whichever is less, it's a really bad idea.

First, if you lose your job, you'll have to repay the entire loan by the next tax filing deadline. If you default on your payments, the loan is treated as a premature distribution, so you're hit with a 10% penalty plus income tax on the loan amount.

But all that aside, cashing out your 401(k), even in the form of a loan, robs your future self of years of returns. Not only that, research shows that most people who borrow from their 401(k) either temporarily stop or reduce their normal contributions while they pay back the loan. It's a double whammy.

Borrowing money from your retirement account usually ends up being the most expensive loan you'll ever make. If your 401(k) is your only source of down payment money, consider putting off homeownership for a while until you can save a bit more.

KEY TAKEAWAYS:

- Most lenders limit total housing costs to 28% of your gross income—that includes taxes, insurance, and condo, co-op or HOA fees.
- You don't have to spend as much as the bank approves you for. A good rule of thumb is to keep your housing payments around 25% of your take-home pay.
- It's best to put 20% down if you want to get the best terms and avoid expensive PMI premiums.
- If you have to borrow your down payment, you may not really be ready to buy a home.

CHAPTER 4.

MORTGAGE 101: EVERYTHING YOU NEED TO KNOW ABOUT FINANCING A HOUSE

A home loan is probably the largest, most long-term financial commitment you'll ever make, so it's a good idea to really understand what you're getting into. Even if homeownership is months in the future, it's never too soon to learn how the mortgage process works and what you can do to get the best deal when you're ready to buy.

(If you're unsure about any terms used in this section, there's a handy glossary of common mortgage terms at the end of the book.)

SURPRISE! A MORTGAGE IS *NOT* THE SAME AS A HOME LOAN

Most people use the word "mortgage" interchangeably with "home loan," but they are two different things. "Mortgage," which comes from the Latin for "death pledge," is the term for the legal instrument giving your lender the right to your property if you default on your loan.

Your lender files a copy of the mortgage with the county recorder as a lien, or claim, on your home. Once the loan is paid off, the lender releases the mortgage lien.

Your home loan, on the other hand, is a promissory note that establishes the amount you're borrowing, the interest rate and repayment terms, and other conditions of the loan. When you finance a home, your mortgage and your promissory note go hand-in-hand.

Some states use deeds of trust instead of mortgages to secure home loans. It's a minor point of difference that only comes into play if you default on your loan and the lender forecloses. Loans secured by a mortgage require judicial foreclosure through the state court system, while those secured by deeds of trust can be foreclosed without a judicial proceeding.

> **New York Note**: New York is a mortgage state that requires a judicial foreclosure process.

HOW MUCH MORTGAGE DO YOU QUALIFY FOR?

Lenders look at several different factors in making mortgage loans:

- Your credit score
- Your income
- Your debt-to-income ratio
- Your down payment

These factors carry different weights and work together to help the lender determine your ability to pay back the loan. For example, a great credit score won't cancel out excessive debt in your lender's eyes, but a big down payment may tip the scales in your favor if your credit score is less than perfect or your income is low.

Generally speaking, if you have adequate, stable income, good credit, low debt, and a 20% down payment, you'll qualify for a mortgage payment of up to 28% of your gross monthly income.

But don't take that number to the bank—there are a lot of things that can affect the final amount your lender approves. It's a good idea to pre-qualify with a lender before you even start the homebuying process.

WHAT'S THE DIFFERENCE BETWEEN PREQUALIFICATION AND PRE-APPROVAL?

Prequalification is an informal process; it's not binding on your lender. Basically, you give your bank or broker information about your income, debts, and assets, and he or she gives you a rough idea of how much home you can afford. In many cases, you can do this online or over the phone.

Prequalification is a very preliminary process, but it can be very enlightening if you're just starting to think about buying a home.

Pre-approval is a much more formal process. You actually fill out a loan application and provide documents such as tax returns, pay stubs, and bank statements. The lender checks your credit, as well.

If all goes well, you get a conditional commitment from the lender, in the form of a pre-approval letter, to provide financing up to a certain amount, as long as nothing changes in your financial situation.

Pre-approval letters give you a leg up in the buying process because they suggest to the seller that you're serious about the offer—and able to close the deal if it's accepted.

Keep in mind that pre-approval is not a guarantee that the loan will close. Your loan package goes to the underwriter, and underwriting is a notoriously tricky process with lots of moving parts. Pre-approval suggests the bank thinks you stand a good chance of surviving the process.

New York Note: If you have your eye on a particular building, it's a good idea to find out which banks lend on those buildings. Certain banks pre-approve certain buildings, but not others. Ask your realtor which banks make loans on any building you're making an offer on to save yourself time and aggravation when applying for a loan.

ARE MORTGAGE RATES BASED ON CREDIT SCORES?

When you apply for a home loan, your credit score is one of the most important factors your lender considers in approving a loan and determining your terms.

Although lenders often use their own scoring models, your FICO score is a good estimator of your creditworthiness. FICO uses a scale of 300 to 850; the average score right now is about 700. Most lenders won't make mortgage loans to people with credit scores below 620, although there are some government-backed programs, such as VA and FHA loans, that approve loans for people with lower scores.

Generally speaking, the higher your credit score, the lower your interest rates. And when you're dealing with a loan of hundreds of thousands of dollars for 20 or 30 years, even a fraction of a percent makes a huge difference. Check out the finance costs for a $500,000, 30-year fixed home loan:

FICO Score	Interest Rate	Interest Paid
760 and above	4.15%	$375,000
700 to 759	4.40%	$401,500
680 to 699	4.75%	$440,000
660 to 679	5.05%	$472,000
640 to 659	5.35%	$505,000
620 to 639	5.95%	$573,000

Interest rates make a huge difference in your monthly principal and interest payment, too. In the mortgage example above, your payment would be nearly $3,000 a month with a 620 credit score, but just $2,400 with a 760 FICO.

ARE THERE DIFFERENT TYPES OF MORTGAGE HOME LOANS?

Depending on your financial situation, your lender, and the type of property you're buying, you may encounter several different terms. The most common ones to know include:

- **Fixed-rate mortgage loans**. As the name implies, you pay the same interest rate for the life of the loan. Fixed-rate loans are usually offered in 15-year, 20-year, and 30-year terms, with 15 and 30 being most common.
- **Adjustable-rate mortgage (ARM)**. ARMs are loans with interest rates pegged to an underlying index, typically the London Interbank Offered Rate (LIBOR) or cost of funds index (COFI). The lender adds a fixed percentage, known as a margin, to the index to determine your loan's interest rate. Margins are generally between 1% and 2%. Adjustable rate mortgages usually offer a lower introductory rate for a fixed period, and then adjust it on an annual basis. A 5/1 ARM has a five-year fixed period and then adjusts on an annual basis. A 7/1 has a seven-year fixed period and then adjusts on an annual basis. ARMs generally have interest rate caps that limit the

amount your interest rate can rise each year, and
also over the life of the loan, to protect you from
huge swings.

- **Conventional loans.** These loans are not backed
  by any government programs. You generally need
  20% down, although some lenders will approve a
  loan with a lower down payment and private
  mortgage insurance.

- **VA, FHA, and USDA loans.** These loans are
  insured by the federal government and you must
  meet certain requirements in order to apply.

- **Conforming loans.** These loans meet the
  underwriting standards of Fannie Mae and Freddie
  Mac, the government entities that buy mortgage-
  backed loans, package them up, and sell them to
  investors.

- **Jumbo loans.** These loans are in amounts that
  exceed the limits for a conforming loan. They
  generally have stricter underwriting requirements.
  The jumbo loan ceiling differs depending on
  where you live.

The mortgage underwriting requirements may be different
for the different types of loans. When you meet with a
lender, he or she will explain your options based on your
finances and the property you're trying to buy.

BANK OR MORTGAGE BROKER: WHICH ONE IS BEST?

It depends. Banks and brokers work very differently.
When you apply for a home loan with a bank, your loan

officer, loan processor, and underwriter are all employees of the financial institution, and the loan is funded with the bank's assets. The bank can either keep your loan in its own portfolio or sell it to investors at any time.

Banks and credit unions generally offer a limited number of mortgage loan products, but they are usually more than adequate for borrowers with good credit and a solid down payment. In many cases, bank loans close more quickly than broker mortgages, and you may have more input and control over the process.

Mortgage brokers, on the other hand, are middlemen. They have relationships with many different wholesale lenders, which means they have access to many different types of loan products. If your financial situation is less straightforward, or you need complex financing, a broker may be able to find a loan when traditional banks and credit unions can't.

Loans arranged by mortgage brokers can be more expensive than a bank loan, but brokers have to disclose their compensation in the closing statement. Sometimes brokers are paid by the lenders in the form of rebates. This is usually the case for higher-rate loans. For more conventional loans, the borrower pays the broker's commission, which usually runs about 1% of the loan amount.

HOW TO COMPARE MORTGAGES

Unless you have a long-standing relationship with a bank or financial institution, or have another compelling reason to use one particular lender, it's a good idea to comparison-shop for a home loan. Because a mortgage loan with Bank A is functionally the same as a mortgage loan at Bank B, the only real difference between the two is the price.

There are three things to consider in comparing mortgage costs:

- Interest rate
- Points
- Closing costs

The interest rate is the annual percentage rate, or APR, you're charged for the privilege of borrowing money.

Points are fees equal to 1% of the loan amount. One point on a $500,000 mortgage would be $5,000. Although some lenders use points to price loan-processing fees, points are most commonly used to "buy down" the interest rate on your mortgage.

For example, Lender A may offer you a $500,000, 30-year fixed mortgage at 4.75% with two points. Lender B offers you the same loan at 5.25% with no points. How do you know which is cheaper? You have to do the math.

Principal and interest on Loan A is $2,608 per month. On Loan B, it's $2,761, a difference of about $150 per month. Two points on Loan A cost $10,000. If you save $150 a month, it would take you five and a half years to recoup the cost of the points you paid for the lower interest rate.

If you plan to stay in your home longer than five and a half years, you're better off buying down your rate with Lender A.

When it comes to closing costs, it pays to compare. Mortgage loan closing costs typically run between 2% and 5% of the loan amount. While some of the fees are fixed, such as appraisal, inspection, and title fees, others are discretionary, such as application, origination, processing, and funding fees. Ask prospective lenders for an estimate of closing costs before you make your decision.

New York Note: New York has an extremely high recording tax, which may drive your closing costs above the 2% to 5% average in other areas.

KEY TAKEAWAYS:

- Good credit is important, but you also need stable income, low debt, and a good down payment to get a mortgage.
- You should definitely comparison-shop to get the best rates on your home loan.
- You should prequalify for a mortgage before you even think of homebuying, and get pre-approved once you're ready to shop.
- Banks are great for most conventional mortgage needs, but if you have complex lending needs, a mortgage broker may be able to find you a loan.

CHAPTER 5.

DECIDING WHERE YOU WANT TO LIVE

This may be stating the obvious, but before you think about square footage, number of bedrooms, and what you want in your perfect kitchen, you need to decide *where* you want to live. After all, you can change a lot of things about your house, but *location* isn't one of them.

Unfortunately, real life isn't like *HGTV* where you (and your homebuying partner, if you have one) magically discover the perfect place to live on your first time out. In most cases, choosing a home location is a purposeful process of elimination that involves painstakingly visiting and narrowing down neighborhoods until you find one you can be happy in. There *will* be compromises along the way.

But one thing's for sure: you will never really *love* your home if you don't love your neighborhood.

Here are some of the most important things to think about before you shop for a place to call home.

WHAT TYPE OF HOME DO YOU WANT?

Do you see yourself in a single family home? A townhouse with a deck or terrace and a fenced yard? Or is a condo or apartment more your style?

Is your dream home in a charming, historic area with lots of mature trees and public parks? If so, be prepared for strict community associations and arcane rules.

On the other hand, if you picture a sleek, modern apartment in a brand new development, you may wind up farther from the center of the city and the amenities most city dwellers crave.

You need to have a concrete vision of the type of property you want to live in before you can search for the right place to buy it.

ARE THERE NEIGHBORHOOD FEATURES YOU CAN'T LIVE WITHOUT?

Think about how you live right now—and the lifestyle you aspire to over the next few years—and narrow down what's important to you. Consider things like privacy, community, walkability, ease of commute, parking, noise, proximity to parks, shopping, restaurants, and cultural amenities. Will the neighborhood support your lifestyle, now and in the future?

> **New York Note**: If you're looking at buildings in the city, amenities vary wildly, but there are some you should definitely pay attention to:

- Is there a doorman? This is important from a safety point of view, and helpful for holding packages if you order online a lot.
- Is the superintendent good? A bad superintendent will nonchalantly "order parts" while you freeze without heat all winter.
- Is the building pet- friendly? Some have very strict rules, many have "no cats" policies.
- Are there enough elevators? You don't want to be in a building with 500 units and one elevator.
- Do they have other amenities such as a health club or pool?

There are bound to be tradeoffs, and you may never find a neighborhood that checks all your boxes, but don't compromise on your deal breakers. If you're the sort who craves quiet evenings at home with a book, you will never be happy with that fabulous townhouse a block from Frat Row, no matter how much you love the original wood floors and La Cornue range.

DOES IT FEEL SAFE?

This one is a matter of personal opinion. Some people are willing to live in an "edgier" neighborhood if it means an easy commute and proximity to great restaurants and shops. Some people aren't comfortable in anything less than a gated community with private security.

But objective crime rates do matter—both in your insurance premiums and your resale value when you're ready to move. Check out neighborhoods you're interested in using online tools such as AreaVibes or CrimeReports. You can also contact the local police department for detailed information on safety and crime statistics.

> **New York Note**: NYC is unique in that neighborhoods can change drastically in a block or two. And like most areas, sunlight sanitizes—you only get a true feel for safety at night. Map out your common routes, such as to the subway, supermarket, bank, etc. Walk those routes after dark and see if your daily routine feels safe.

HOW ARE THE SCHOOLS?

If you have children, this is going to be a major factor in your decision. But even if you don't, it still matters—you don't want to limit your future buyers to childless people by choosing a home in a poor school district.

Again, there are good online tools such as Schooldigger.com, Greatschools.org, and Education.com that you can use to see how schools in the neighborhood rank. Don't forget to check into daycares and preschools as well. You may come to hate your neighborhood if it's 30 minutes away from your childcare provider.

HOW AFFORDABLE IS THE NEIGHBORHOOD?

If you're pre-qualified for a mortgage payment, you have a good idea of what you can afford. But keep in mind, your monthly payment doesn't just include principal and interest—it includes property taxes, homeowners insurance, and any HOA, co-op, or condo fees as well. Those costs alone can eat up half your budget.

Beyond those fixed expenses, however, you have to consider other costs of living. What is the cost of your commute—in both time and money? Are the nearby restaurants, grocery stores, retail shops, and service providers within your typical budget category, or significantly higher that what you usually spend?

If you're used to working out at the local Y for $70 a month, will you keep up your routine when the neighborhood fitness club costs $350 a month?

LIVING IN THE CITY VERSUS THE SUBURBS

Few things make a bigger impact on your quality of life than the choice between living in the city or the 'burbs— and there are lots of factors to consider before you make that choice:

- **Commuting**. If you work in the city and live in the suburbs, you'll have a commute. Even if there's public transportation part of the way, you'll probably have to drive to the station and pay to park your car. You may be able to get by without a car if you live in the city, but in the suburbs, that's probably not an option. Consider your costs accordingly.
- **Size and type of home.** Life in the suburbs is great if you picture yourself in a single family home with a couple of kids, a big yard, and a boisterous dog or two. It's also great if the

thought of home renovation excites you—you'll have more control to change or expand your property. On the other hand, if lawn maintenance and home repairs aren't your thing, a brownstone or condo in the city might be more your style.

- **Diversity.** The suburbs have a reputation as a homogenous haven for the middle class, although those trends are changing in recent years. There's more diversity in the suburbs than in the past, but generally speaking, city dwellers are a much more diverse bunch.

- **Culture and recreation.** It's often said that suburbs are great for parks and outdoor recreation, but short on the museums, galleries, performing arts venues, and restaurants that make life in the city exciting. Although that's not always the case, it's more accurate than not most of the time.

- **Education.** No one likes to state the obvious, but public schools are funded by property taxes, so suburban school districts tend to have more money than city schools. This isn't always the case, but for the most part, kids get a higher quality education in the suburbs, unless you're sending them off to private school.

New York Note: NYC is a conspicuous exception when it comes to public schools, with many of the most competitive and prestigious public schools in the world located in the five boroughs. However, admission can be a byzantine maze of testing, ranking, and lotteries, instead of the simpler suburban process of just living in the zone.

INDICATORS YOU'VE FOUND A GOOD NEIGHBORHOOD

After you've narrowed down general areas and made the city versus suburbs decision, how do you choose between several different neighborhoods that potentially meet your needs?

Here are some things that differentiate acceptable neighborhoods from great neighborhoods, especially from a financial point of view.

Look for more homeowners than renters

In the US, the average neighborhood has roughly two homeowners for each renter, but you're better off in neighborhoods where a higher percentage of residents are homeowners. People who own their homes tend to put more time, effort, and money into maintenance, which means higher home values in the neighborhood as a whole. Industry experts advise against buying in neighborhoods where more than 25% are rental homes.

Keep an eye out for emerging neighborhoods

Check price trends for homes and apartment buildings over the past two to three years, especially for properties that have recently sold. Are they selling above or below the asking price? Do they stay on the market for more than 30 days? Don't look at "average sales price" data for the neighborhood—granular information about specific properties similar to one you'd like to buy is more important.

There are other indicators a neighborhood is about to take off and it's a good place to buy:

- A new business is opening up, bringing an influx of new jobs
- Lots of new construction and/or home renovations are underway
- There is expansion of public transportation to a neighborhood that was previously unserved
- New retail development is occurring

Watch the path of growth
Cities tend to grow in predictable patterns and cycles. When one neighborhood takes off and buyers are priced out, the neighborhoods closest to it become more desirable. If you move into an amenity-rich neighborhood on the cusp of the growth cycle, you could see much higher-than-average increases in home values over time.

Pay attention to absorption rates
This is a fancy term for the ratio of the number of neighborhood listings in a given month and the number of sales during the same month. An upward-trending absorption rate suggests the neighborhood is heating up and will likely provide better value for your money than one with a downward-trending or low absorption rate, regardless of whether you're in a buyer's or seller's market.

Check into development plans
This is important for a couple of reasons. First of all, the average homeowner stays in a house for 10 years before selling. If you're 35 right now, can you see yourself living happily in the neighborhood when you're 45? If not, does

the city have commercial development plans in place for the area that might change your opinion?

Secondly, if you're not planning to stay in a home for 10 years, development plans could affect your ability to sell your house. For example, if you're moving into a newly-built house in a development with several years of construction left, you'll have a hard time selling your home while new homes are being built. Most buyers will bypass your existing home and zero in on something brand new.

GET BEYOND THE STATISTICS

While statistics are a good framework for evaluating a neighborhood, you have to move beyond the math and into the street. Set up "dates" with neighborhoods you like at different times of the day—maybe have dinner one night after work to check the traffic patterns and commute, and enjoy brunch and a stroll on a Sunday afternoon to experience the weekend ambiance.

The idea is to see how the neighborhood feels and aligns with your lifestyle. Are there people on the street and do they seem friendly? Is there pride of ownership in the homes? Does it feel comfortable after dark? Is the noise level tolerable? Do you see yourself fitting in—and flourishing—in this environment?

It bears repeating: if you don't love your neighborhood, you'll never be happy in your home.

WHAT HAPPENS WHEN COUPLES DISAGREE ABOUT WHERE TO LIVE?

If you see a dream home and your partner sees a nightmare, it can feel like you'll never agree on a place to live. Try these tips to help you reach an agreement:

- **Go easy on the deal breakers**. You and your partner should list just two or three non-negotiables each and agree in advance to eliminate any neighborhood that violates either of your deal breakers. Then be willing to compromise in good faith on everything else.

- **Prioritize your preferences.** Rank your preferred features in order, and have your partner do the same. If a particular neighborhood doesn't deliver on at least three of your top priorities, for both you and your partner, exclude it from consideration.

- **Don't rely on emotion.** Buying a home is an emotional process, but your feelings shouldn't be the only (or primary) consideration. Make a fact-based case for a particular neighborhood you love—and consider your partner's fact-based case against it. Facts don't lie, and they may help make the best choice obvious.

- **Consult a professional.** A good real estate agent can give you unbiased views about different neighborhoods you like and can often suggest a solution you hadn't considered that works well for both of you.

If you still can't agree, consider postponing the search. If you've spent a few weeks or months looking and nothing pleases you both, put house hunting on the backburner for a while. It's better than digging in and letting disagreements unravel your relationship.

KEY TAKEAWAYS:

- The *type* of home you want sets the stage for choosing where to live. Decide that first.
- Make sure your neighborhood is a place you'll be happy living in 10 years from now.
- Suburban living is generally much cheaper than living in the city, but there are a lot of tradeoffs to consider.
- If a home is an investment, it makes sense to choose your location with price growth in mind.

CHAPTER 6.

SHOPPING FOR—AND CHOOSING—YOUR FIRST HOME

Shopping for your first house can be one of life's greatest thrills...or it can be a struggle of biblical proportions. Although there's not much you can do if the market is tight and the sellers are smug, having the right attitude and a solid plan of attack goes a long way toward finding your dream home without losing your mind.

Assuming you've done the hard stuff—set your budget, been pre-approved for a loan, and nailed down acceptable locations—house hunting itself is fairly easy. The Internet is an amazing time-saver, especially if you're shopping with a partner. Looking online first can help eliminate those homes you'll never agree on so you don't waste time touring properties you'll never buy.

One tip before you start: curb your enthusiasm. You need a healthy dose of detachment to accurately evaluate a home. If you view your first home as the single most important purchase you'll ever make, then you know how critical it is to get it right. Approach it objectively, and don't let your heart overrule your head. It's much easier to recover from a $500 impulse purchase than a $500,000 one. Shop wisely.

KNOW THE DIFFERENCE BETWEEN NEEDS AND WANTS

Here's a painful truth about your first home: you will never find one that perfectly matches the dream home of your imagination.

But you *will* find one that has everything you need—and quite possibly most of the things you want. The trick is knowing where to compromise.

Make a list of your housing must-haves. Think about living space, storage, and structural features that can't be easily changed after you buy.

From there, add in nice-to-have features you're willing to pay for, such as granite countertops, hardwood floors, or oversized windows with a wonderful view.

Spend a moment thinking about deal breakers, and add them to the list. Why is this important? Too many first-time buyers fall in love with a home that meets all their needs and wants, but has *one glaring flaw*. They get caught up in the wave of excitement and believe all the other great features will make up for that one fatal flaw.

Once the new homeowners move in, reality hits. That glaring flaw makes them miserable with their new house after a month or two. If you spot a non-negotiable in an otherwise perfect home, do yourself a favor and just *walk away*.

NARROW DOWN YOUR SEARCH ONLINE

The Internet is a homebuyer's best friend. With a few clicks, you can set search parameters and sift through hundreds of listings to find the best fits. Most sites offer virtual tours as well, saving you the aggravation of visiting homes you know aren't right for you.

Do remember, though, that pictures never tell the whole story. In fact, the best-looking listings aren't always the best homes. Agents aren't going to feature the cracked flooring or ancient water heater in their photos and videos, so pay attention to the detailed listing information about the property's age and other essential features.

Keep in mind that not all real estate sites are equally helpful. Some don't update often enough to offer current information. Others limit listings to those with particular brokers. Some of the best are Zillow, Redfin, Trulia, and Realtor.com.

New York Note: The best site for finding apartment buildings in New York and the outer boroughs is StreetEasy. Zillow is best for other types of properties.

DON'T RUSH THE PROCESS

The average first-time homebuyer finds a suitable home within two weeks of visiting his or her first property. That's the good news.

The bad news is that an "average homebuyer" is like a unicorn—it doesn't really exist. You might have a budget that severely limits your choice of homes; you may need certain hard-to-find features; or you may be searching in a neighborhood or building where new listings are few and far between.

Give yourself ample time and flexibility to shop for the best fit given your current situation. If that means you don't make an offer for 60 days, it's not the end of the world. Better to take your time and buy wisely than jump into a house you'll regret.

TAKE ADVANTAGE OF OPEN HOUSES

Touring open homes is an excellent learning experience and great preparation for visiting the home you eventually want to buy. Before you start shopping in earnest, it's a good idea to set aside a couple of weekends to visit a variety of open houses, even if they're not exactly the type of home or location you're looking for.

There are a lot of advantages to doing so:

- Looking at layouts, features, and fundamentals of different homes in person helps you identify and prioritize the things you really want in your own home.
- You learn to filter out the nonessentials that shouldn't impact your evaluation of a home. For example, you no longer equate great staging with a great home, or see an ugly paint color as a deal-breaking flaw.

- You're no longer wowed by flashy upgrades, and you zero in on things like natural light, ventilation and air flow, and structural soundness that are key to a good home.
- You get a much better appreciation for home pricing—you'll be better equipped to recognize a fair home price and an unrealistic one.

Use open houses as a way to spruce up on your home inspection and evaluation skills. Use this mental checklist to help you focus on the important things:

❏ Are there signs of water damage along the floors, baseboards, ceilings, or cabinets under the sinks?

❏ Are exposed pipes dry and in good condition?

❏ Are the windows oriented to let in sunlight? Are the views pleasing? Are windows and doors free of drafts?

❏ Are there lots of rugs on the floor? Discreetly pull them back to check the condition of the floors underneath.

❏ Are there adequate electrical outlets and are they conveniently placed?

❏ Are any appliances included with the home in good condition and well-maintained?

❏ Is there adequate, conveniently placed storage?

❏ Do the neighbors maintain their homes and yards?

❏ Is the home arranged for privacy? Is there adequate space between your windows and your neighbors'? Is there excessive noise?

❏ Does the home pass the smell test? Do you detect any musty odors, pet urine, smoke, or other unpleasant smells?

❏ Do all functional windows open easily and show no signs of condensation or moisture?

❏ Is there good ventilation in the kitchen and bathrooms?

❏ Is the exterior of the home in good repair and without evidence of foundation problems?

Do observe good homebuyer etiquette when you're visiting open homes—especially when you're touring one you may eventually want to buy. After all, a good first impression sets the stage for a better buying experience. Here are a few do's and don'ts:

- DO dress appropriately and be prepared to remove your shoes if asked
- DO leave kids and pets at home
- DO feel free to walk in without knocking or ringing the bell (unless there's a sign saying otherwise)
- DO sign in and/or introduce yourself to the seller's agent
- DON'T enter rooms until other visitors have vacated them
- DON'T open any closed doors to rooms without asking first
- DO feel free to look in closets and open drawers or doors of any built-in kitchen and bathroom cabinets, but leave the owner's free-standing furniture alone

- DO bring any obvious issues to the agent's attention

If you're visiting an open house for a property you're interested in buying, pay attention to what the other visitors are saying and doing. You may pick up on an issue or special feature that you overlooked. If the open house is poorly attended, or people don't stay long or leave after viewing a room or two, it may indicate that the house is a dud. On the other hand, if people linger and engage the agent in conversation, it could suggest that an offer will be forthcoming.

FIND A GOOD AGENT WHEN YOU'RE SERIOUS ABOUT SHOPPING

You will want representation when you're actually ready to buy your home. You can do preliminary browsing, visit open houses, and scour online listings on your own, but when the time comes to actually choose and make an offer on a home, you need a good agent.

Your realtor has deeper insight into available homes and information about trends in the areas you're interested in—and can alert you to a hot new listing you might not otherwise have seen. He or she can help you narrow down your possibilities so you don't waste time looking at properties that won't meet your needs and financial ability.

Your realtor is also your liaison with the seller. He schedules appointments, gathers useful information about the homes you visit, and serves as a helpful buffer between you and the seller. If you ever want to see a home without the sellers watching your every move, you'll *definitely* want a realtor.

New York Note: In NYC, agents not only specialize in neighborhoods within the boroughs (e.g., Hell's Kitchen, Brooklyn Heights, Long Island City), they can even be hyper-specialized, focusing on just one building. This is both good and bad: a realtor can have great inside knowledge about, and relationships with, the condo or co-op board, but may lack broader perspective about the real estate market as a whole. Before you choose an NYC realtor, consider those areas of specialization and expertise, but don't make your decision on that basis alone.

KNOW THE SECRETS FOR SUCCESSFUL SHOWINGS

Once you've got a short list of possible homes, your realtor will schedule appointments for you. Ideally, you'll see several homes in a single day, although you might see the odd house on an individual basis if a new listing with great potential turns up.

Limit yourself to six or seven showings at a time—after that, you can go into sensory overload and all of the details can run together.

Conventional wisdom says you should bring a camera and take plenty of pictures and extensive notes at each home you visit, but that can actually backfire. You might be so busy documenting the property that you don't organically experience it and end up missing important details. Besides, most of the information you need will be on the seller's brochure or online description of the property.

After you visit a home, rate it on a scale of 1 to 10. Make a few brief notes about features you really liked and ones that gave you pause.

SCHEDULE A REPEAT VISIT

After a few house-hunting trips, you'll instinctively know which homes you can see yourself buying. Ask your realtor to schedule a second visit with those top prospects. A good realtor knows you'll need more time on a second visit and will make plans accordingly.

Your realtor should also bring more detailed financial information for each of the homes you visit a second time. Ask to see "comps" (comparative financial details) for similar homes in the neighborhood. Find out how long the house has been on the market and whether the price has changed to see if the seller is particularly motivated. Get information about any major renovations or repairs over the last few years.

Take your time during the second visit to really "get under the hood," so to speak. This visit is all about the details, so you may want to bring an experienced friend or family member, or even a contractor, with you this time. You want fresh eyes and a neutral opinion—you already know what you love about the house, so it's time to look for the flaws.

Check the lighting in each room and the condition and age of the fixtures. If overhead fixtures and ceiling fans aren't currently installed, check whether the rooms are wired for them. Check the water pressure in the shower and sinks: turn them on at the same time and see if the pressure changes. Make sure the appliances are in good shape and operational.

Signs of deferred maintenance should give you pause. A homeowner who neglects routine maintenance is more likely to ignore the bigger issues. Look for leaky faucets, burned-out lightbulbs, shabby grout, a dirty fireplace—anything that suggests neglect.

Make a note of any issues you discover. You'll want to account for them in your offer, if you decide to make one.

THE APARTMENT BUYER'S CHECKLIST

If you're buying a condo or co-op, you've got not just your individual unit to consider, but the rest of the building as well. When you're ready for the second visit, be sure you've gone over every item on this checklist before you make an offer.

- ❑ Are common areas clean and well-maintained?
- ❑ Are noise levels acceptable? Consider street noise through windows, footsteps from neighbors above, and sounds of side neighbors through the walls.
- ❑ Is there adequate natural light? How many hours of sunlight does the unit get?

❏ Are you clear on what's included in your unit, such as reserved parking and storage?

❏ Do you know what your association fees include?

❏ Are there adequate elevators, especially during rush hour?

❏ Are the heating and air conditioning centrally controlled? If so, when are the units switched over?

❏ What are the delivery policies? Can take-out meals be delivered to your door or do you have to go down to get them? Are any types of deliveries banned?

❏ Have you seen a copy of the house rules?

❏ What is the smoking policy? If neighbors smoke, the smell can seep through apartment walls more easily than you might expect.

❏ Has the building had any bedbugs or other infestations within the last year?

❏ How is trash disposed of?

❏ Is the building more than 50% sponsor or developer-owned? If so, you have less input on key decisions about your home.

❏ Do you know the sublet policy?

❏ Are there any special restrictions you should be aware of?

❏ Who maintains and manages the building?

❏ Are there any special assessments planned?

KEY TAKEAWAYS:

- The average homebuyer makes an offer on a home within two weeks of visiting the first property, but don't be discouraged if it takes two months in a tight housing market.
- Open houses are great for learning how to evaluate a potential home. Visit as many as you can, even those that you aren't really interested in buying.
- A second set of eyes can help you spot problems you overlooked in a home you really love.

CHAPTER 7.

ASSEMBLING YOUR HOMEBUYING TEAM

The Internet is an amazing thing—you can find out how to do just about anything if you know how to use the Google.

The downside to this, however, is that all this free online knowledge gives people the mistaken idea that they are suddenly experts at a particular thing. It might be okay to rely on your Internet expertise if all you're doing is trying to repair a leaky faucet—you can always call a plumber if you get stuck.

But relying on Internet expertise is a terrible idea when you're buying a house. A lack of professional knowledge can have devastating—and lasting—financial consequences.

If you're ready to take the next step toward homeownership, there are a few professionals you'll need on your side.

CAN I BUY A HOME WITHOUT A REALTOR?

You could, but why would you? As a buyer, it typically costs you nothing out-of-pocket to enlist the services of a realtor; the fees are paid at closing. And a good realtor is an invaluable asset, especially for first-time homebuyers.

Here's a list of services you should expert from a buyer's agent:

- **Help you get pre-approved for a home loan**. Most people are well-advised to mortgage-shop and choose the lender with the lowest fees and best rates. If you're using conventional financing to purchase your first home, you may not need a realtor's help to get pre-approval.

  But if you have unusual or complex financing needs, a realtor may be able to connect you with a mortgage broker or other lender offering creative or non-conforming loan products.

  Do keep in mind, however, that just because your realtor has a relationship with a particular lender, or recommends a broker or bank, you aren't obligated to use them.

  > **New York Note**: In NYC, some banks pre-approve certain buildings. If you have a building in mind, your realtor should know which lenders make mortgage loans on those units and help you negotiate that process.

- **Give you unbiased information on, and make recommendations about, neighborhoods in general and specific properties in particular.** If you don't have a specific neighborhood or building in mind, a good realtor can offer suggestions based on your needs. He or she should be knowledgeable about schools, zoning issues, crime, development plans, trends in the housing market, and other factors that go into choosing your next home.

New York Note: NY agents are prohibited from advising on the pros and cons of zoned schools. They are limited to naming the zoned school and pointing you to the Department of Education website. So, here are some resources for learning about the quality of schools on your own: https://www.schools.nyc.gov/about-us/reports/school-quality, https://insideschools.org, http://www.nyccharterschools.org, https://www.parentsleague.org.

If you've already made a decision about where you want to buy, your realtor can help you filter through the available properties to find the best buys.

New York Note: Some agents in NYC are hyper-specialized and focus on a specific building or buildings.

- **Tour homes with you.** You can drive by homes for sale and tour open houses on your own, but to actually get inside for a private showing, you'll need a realtor. Your realtor handles all the phone calls and makes the appointments—and usually chauffeurs you around from home to home.

- **Help you negotiate a contract.** A good realtor will have expert knowledge about all of the factors that affect the value of the property you want to buy. He or she will know a realistic bottom-line sales figure for the home and advise you on a strategy to negotiate the best possible price.

  Keep in mind, your offer (and the final contract) includes far more than just the price you want to pay for the home. An agent will help you with all of the other details, such as: the earnest money amount (and what happens to it if the offer is rejected or you can't complete the deal), your closing date, how expenses will be prorated at closing, who will pay the various closing costs, and contingencies for inspections, financing, appraisal, and repairs.

- **Be involved in the home inspection process.** You can probably find a competent home inspector on your own, but a good agent knows from experience which ones are best at giving you the true picture of any property you want to buy. This is one area where a realtor's advice definitely matters. You should also take your realtor's advice about other inspections that may affect your home, such as mold, radon, and lead paint.

  You'll also want your real estate agent to attend any home inspections to hear firsthand any issues the inspector finds. He or she can then explain them to you and help you figure out which things should be brought to the seller's attention for negotiation.

Some realtors don't automatically attend inspections, but you can and should insist that your agent be there. Remember, your real estate agent is working for you—and is taking home a big chunk of money for representing you. It's not unreasonable for you to have expectations about the services you get from your realtor.

> **New York Note**: Condo and co-op apartments usually don't have inspections, but your agent will help you with the board application, interview, and approval process—which is often as onerous as the mortgage application process.

- **Monitor and expedite the closing process**. Once a contract is finalized, a lot of moving pieces come into play. Your realtor functions as a communications hub between you, your lender, your closing attorney, the seller's agent, the inspector, and all the other people involved in finalizing the deal.

HOW DO I CHOOSE A REALTOR?

A word of caution before you even start the realtor selection process: make sure you're truly ready to buy. Real estate agents and brokers work on commission, meaning they don't get paid until you close on a house. If you aren't qualified and prepared to actually buy a home, it's unfair to waste a real estate agent's time.

Know your terms

A **real estate agent** is someone who has taken some basic educational classes and passed a state licensing exam. In some states, the word "salesperson" is used instead of agent. Whatever they are called, these professionals can only work under the supervision of a licensed real estate broker. They are not able to hang a shingle and open a real estate business on their own.

A **real estate broker**, on the other hand, has more education specific to real estate and has passed the broker licensing exam. Brokers can open their own offices and hire agents or salespeople to work for them. They usually have to take continuing education and may have to comply with other state requirements in order to maintain their licenses.

Interestingly, the term "**realtor**" is actually a registered trademark of the National Association of REALTORS. A real estate agent can't legally be called a realtor unless he's a paid-up member of the association and follows the NAR's code of ethics.

The **listing agent** acts on behalf of the seller and has a fiduciary responsibility to the seller. In other words, under the terms of the listing agreement, the listing agent's first duty is to protect the seller's interest.

The **selling agent** can also be referred to as the buyer's agent, but to be clear, ALL parties in the real estate transaction technically represent the seller. Once a buyer-broker agreement is signed, however, the selling agent owes fiduciary responsibility to the buyer.

A **buyer's agent** prefers to work only with buyers. There is no specific licensure required for buyer's agents, although the NAR does have Accredited Buyer Representative (ABR) designation for agents who complete the requisite coursework and licensing exam. Some first-time homebuyers prefer to work with exclusive buyer's agents.

Dual agency occurs when a single agent represents both the buyer and the seller, or even when both the listing agent and selling agent work for the same broker. Not all states allow dual agency. In states where dual agency is illegal, an agent can become a **transaction agent**, who represents neither the buyer nor the seller, but impartially facilitates the real estate transaction.

New York Note: In NY, listing and seller's agent are synonymous. The buyer's agent is whoever brings the buyer (you) to the deal. A dual agency is when the listing/selling agent also finds you the buyer through an open house, for example, and then represents both sides.

Get referrals

Unless you live in a very small town, you likely have your choice of hundreds of real estate professionals. A good way to narrow down your selection is with a recommendation from a trusted friend or colleague.

You can also look at real estate signs on homes in the neighborhoods you're interested in. Those agents likely have experience in, and knowledge of, the area where you want to buy.

Conduct interviews

Yes, you really should interview at least three agents before you sign an agreement with one (more on that later). If you don't have great rapport with any of the three, be prepared to interview more.

Some questions to ask:

- How long have you been in real estate and what is your license number?
- Do you do real estate work full-time or part-time?
- Do you specialize in working with buyers?
- How many transactions do you typically complete in a month?
- What neighborhoods do you focus on?
- How do I communicate with you? What's your typical response time to emails, phone calls, texts?

Ultimately, though, the choice of an agent usually comes down to chemistry and rapport. If you find a realtor that checks all your credentials and experience boxes but rubs you the wrong way, move on and find one you like and feel you can trust.

Sign a buyer-broker agreement and agency agreement

These documents formalize the relationship between you and the agent and establish the agent's fiduciary responsibility to you. Every state requires an agency disclosure document for buyers, although the exact nature of the document varies from state to state.

The agent's fiduciary responsibility to buyers gives you important rights and protections. For example, it is a breach of fiduciary for the agent to do anything to undermine your offer to the seller. Suppose you ask your agent to submit a low-ball offer on a house, and when he delivers it to the listing agent, he mentions that you could afford to go much higher.

Or, imagine that the home inspection uncovers several issues that you want the seller to repair, but your agent tells the listing agent that you're motivated to get the deal done, and if the seller counters with an offer to repair only the most significant issue, you'll probably take it. Both of these examples are illegal abuses of fiduciary duty.

Broker agreements can be exclusive or non-exclusive; there are pros and cons to both. If you sign an exclusive agreement, you can only work with that agent during the time the agreement is in force. On the other hand, you can have non-exclusive agreements with as many different agents as you like. Whatever agreement you sign, make sure your agent will release you from it if you are unhappy with the services he or she provides. If not, don't hire that agent.

WHY YOU NEED A REAL ESTATE ATTORNEY

First of all, if you live in one of the following states, you are *required* to have a real estate attorney involved in the closing process:

- Alabama
- Connecticut
- Delaware
- District of Columbia
- Florida
- Georgia
- Kansas
- Kentucky
- Maine
- Maryland
- Massachusetts
- Mississippi
- New Hampshire
- North Carolina
- North Dakota
- New York
- Rhode Island
- South Carolina
- Vermont
- Virginia
- West Virginia

But even if you don't live in one of those states, a real estate attorney is an invaluable part of your team, especially if you're a first-time homebuyer. Although most real estate transactions chug along using standardized forms and procedures, there are many different potential situations that simply can't be managed by your agent or lender.

What does a real estate attorney do?

Here's what a real estate attorney's responsibilities might look like for a transaction in New York, for example:

- The seller's attorney prepares the sales contract, and you send it to your attorney to review. Your attorney looks for any issues that may need to be addressed, such as whether or not any alterations or additions to the property were made lawfully, and whether the escrow instructions are clear. The attorneys negotiate the final terms of the sales contract, and when everything is approved, you, the buyer, sign the contract and your attorney sends it to the seller with your down payment according to the agreed-upon terms.

> **New York Note**: With condos and co-ops, your buyer's attorney does your due diligence. This means reviewing the condo/co-op board and shareholder meeting minutes, building financials, etc., for any red flags regarding the building's financial health, upcoming capital improvements, or other issues that may affect you in the future.

- Your attorney orders a title report to look for any issues that may affect your ownership of the home. These may include liens, property violations, tax delinquencies, and problems with chain of ownership. He will issue a title opinion and apply for title insurance.

- At the same time, your real estate attorney coordinates with you and your lender to get the appropriate documents, and monitors inspection reports that may affect closing.
- The attorney collects documents from the lender and disclosures from the seller's attorney and prepares a settlement statement showing what you owe at closing to the various parties (seller, seller's lender, title company, etc.)
- Once everything is in order, the attorney represents you at closing, explaining all documents to you, ensuring that the deed, mortgage documents, and transfer tax returns are properly prepared, and making sure all payments are made properly.

Perhaps the real estate attorney's most important role, however, is representing your interests. In a typical real estate transaction, both your agent and the listing agent technically work for the seller (it's the seller who pays their fees, after all), and the seller's attorney is obviously also there to safeguard the seller's interest. In any situation where your interests and the seller's are in conflict, the deck is clearly stacked against you. Even your lender is looking out for the bank's interests, not yours.

That's where your real estate attorney comes in. He or she is the only person in this process who is solely dedicated to watching out for *you*. Every other professional in the deal gets paid only when the deal closes, so they are incentivized to complete the transaction. You pay your attorney no matter what, so she is not financially incentivized to close a deal that isn't in your best interests. For a first-time homebuyer, that peace of mind is invaluable.

HOW DO I HIRE A REAL ESTATE ATTORNEY?

Don't wait to look for a real estate attorney until you're ready to sign a contract. Ideally, you should have a real estate attorney in mind before you hire a real estate agent. You may want a lawyer's advice before you sign any agreements with a real estate agent or broker.

Follow the same general principles you would for hiring any professional service provider:

- Ask for recommendations from friends and colleagues
- Research real estate attorneys online
- Once you narrow down a list of possibilities, request a consultation with at least three possible candidates
- During the consultation, get information on experience, fees, the attorney's record with the state bar, the size of the firm, and what percentage of the practice is devoted to real estate

You won't spend as much face-to-face time with your real estate attorney as you will with your real estate agent, so personality issues are less important. You want a conveniently located attorney who has specific expertise handling your type of real estate transaction and charges a reasonable fee for your area.

HOW MUCH DO REAL ESTATE ATTORNEYS COST?

Attorney fees vary wildly depending on where you live. In some states, you can pay between $500 and $1,500 for a straightforward sale. In New York, average costs range between $1,000 and $4,000 for a real estate transaction.

Find out how your attorney charges for real estate closings. Some charge by the hour and some offer a flat fee to close a transaction.

There are certain factors that affect attorney fees in a real estate transaction, including:

- Cash deals versus financed purchases
- Bank loan versus private lender
- Location of the parties (local or out-of-state)
- Type of property (single-family, condo, co-op, or multi-family)
- Whether a mortgage needs to be paid off
- Any issues affecting the title

Although it's a good idea to price-shop mortgages to cut costs, it's never a good idea to cut corners on your legal representation. Remember, your attorney is the only person in the transaction 100% committed to watching out for your best interests—and this is one area where you get what you pay for.

KEY TAKEAWAYS:

- Since the seller pays all real estate commissions, there's really no reason to buy a home without an agent representing you

- Be sure to sign a buyer-broker agreement with your agent so the agent's fiduciary responsibilities are spelled out.

- Even if you don't live in a state where an attorney is required at closing, keep in mind that your real estate attorney is the only person specifically safeguarding your interests in the real estate deal.

CHAPTER 8.
HOW TO MAKE AN OFFER AND NEGOTIATE A CONTRACT ON YOUR FIRST HOME

All your hard work researching and shopping for homes has finally paid off, and you've found the one you're ready to buy. Things are about to get serious.

The paperwork process for purchasing a home varies depending on where you live. In some places, only a real estate attorney can prepare a purchase contract, and in others, your agent completes the required forms.

But before you sign any documents, you need to know the steps to making a fair offer and negotiating a price and closing conditions.

WHAT'S INVOLVED IN A HOME OFFER?

The offer, or purchase contract, will be different in different parts of the country, but they usually contain similar elements. Common elements include the following, all of which are ultimately negotiable:

- The purchase price of the home
- Who pays fees such as transfer taxes, title insurance, escrow fees, inspection fees, HOA

transfer fees, and disclosure fees that may be required by the state

- How to prorate expenses such as taxes, utilities, insurance
- The amount of earnest money
- Inspections and time period to complete them
- Any personal property to remain in the home
- Any contingencies and the time period to release them, such as selling an existing home
- Time period for disclosures
- Closing costs
- Closing date
- Date of possession

Customs also vary by location. In some areas, it's normal for the buyer to submit a personal letter to the seller along with the purchase contract. This may be helpful in a tight market where several buyers are competing for the same property. Your real estate agent should guide you in this regard.

DETERMINING HOME VALUE AND PURCHASE PRICE OFFER

Most buyers consider the following four things in making an offer on a home:

1. **Are you in a buyer's or seller's market?** If it's a seller's market, you may not have much wiggle room to deviate from the listing price. For particularly desirable properties, it's not

uncommon to have a bidding war when the market is tight.

On the other hand, in a buyer's market, there's more price flexibility. With a high inventory of available homes, sellers seriously consider every offer that comes in. You may be able to knock 10% or more off the home price to open negotiations.

2. **How long has the house been on the market?** Even in a seller's market, you will want to know how long the listing has been active. When a home is newly listed, sellers aren't under any pressure to consider less-than-ideal offers. On the other hand, if a property has been on the market for 90 days and already had a price reduction, you're probably safe going low.

Ask your real estate agent for price and listing history on the home before you arrive at an offer price. Sometimes, listing agents get sneaky with a home that's been on the market for more than a couple of months. To avoid the negative price consequences of an "old" listing, they'll have the seller take the home off the market for a few weeks and then re-list it so it looks like a newly listed home. This will show up in the listing history.

3. **What are comparable homes selling for?** Your agent should provide you with a list of comparables, but you can also use filters on sites

like Zillow and Redfin to get your own comps. You are looking for sales within the last 60 to 90 days on homes very similar to the one you're trying to buy. Depending on the market, you may not be able to find an identical or nearly identical floor plan to the home you're buying. In that case, look at comparable square footage.

Keep in mind that sales price doesn't reflect any financial concessions that the seller got when he or she purchased the home. For example, comps may show that a particular home sold for $500,000, but the seller may have given up $10,000 in closing costs, meaning the true sales price was $490,000. Your agent should check for seller concessions on any comparables you're using to negotiate an offer price.

> **New York Note**: Because NYC has so much inventory and so many transactions, comps can be very specific. Sites like streeteasy.com give great data, showing you recent sales of units in the same building, on the same line (Apt 10A vs Apt 15A), and with the exact same floor plan! So you may have *very* good comp data, with minor adjustments for floor (higher is usually better), view, and interior condition.

4. **How committed are you to buying this particular home?** There's always risk involved in negotiating a home price and concessions. If you feel you won't be happy in any other home, or you'll have lasting regret if you let this deal fall

through, you need to make the proverbial "offer
that can't be refused."

Let your agent advise you on the opening price offer. He
or she has a good idea of what types of offers are usually
accepted on similar properties. You don't have to accept
the agent's price recommendations; however, if you go too
far to get a good deal, you risk offending the seller and
shutting down negotiations entirely. Know how much
you're willing to gamble before you name your offer price.

LET YOUR EARNEST MONEY DO THE TALKING

Local customs dictate earnest deposits to some degree—in
some areas, 1% is normal, and in others, especially tighter
markets, 10% is common. However, nothing
communicates a willingness to negotiate in good faith like
a substantial earnest deposit.

Putting down a minimal amount of earnest money
suggests a low commitment to closing the deal. If you are
sure you want to buy *this particular home* (and seriously, if
you're not, why are you even making an offer?), put down
a significant amount of earnest money, usually 10%.

Keep in mind, however, that there is a *huge* difference
between your **earnest money deposit** and your **down
payment**. The earnest money accompanies your
offer/purchase agreement and is held in escrow until
closing, when it is applied to your down payment or
closing costs. If you back out of the deal for a reason not

covered by contingencies in your purchase contract, you forfeit the earnest money to the seller.

BE SMART ABOUT CONTINGENCIES

Contingencies are the "if this, then that" language of homebuying. For example, "*If* I am able to secure financing within X number of days, *then* I will buy your home," is a common-sense protection that doesn't leave you on the hook if your home loan falls through—and doesn't commit the seller to an extended period of time with the home off the market.

Other contingencies to consider in your offer include:

- **Home inspections**. The offer should stipulate a timeframe for inspection by a qualified home inspector, as well as a timeframe to resolve any required repairs or replacements, or negotiate a resolution or amended contract. Sometimes a seller will want the home to be sold "as is." For you as a buyer, this is extremely risky, because it means the seller is not required to make any repairs regardless of what the home inspection turns up.

- **Appraisal.** Lenders make loans based on a ratio of the loan amount to the home's appraised value. If your appraisal isn't high enough to justify the mortgage amount you need for the agreed-upon price, you need an escape hatch. Of course, you can always negotiate a solution to a low appraisal. The seller can lower the purchase price or you can make up some of the difference in cash. It's not a deal breaker, but you should include the contingency so that you aren't legally obligated to buy at the agreed-upon price.

- **Sale of an existing home**. If you need to sell your current home before you can buy the one you're making an offer on, this needs to be mentioned as a contingency. However, keep in mind that chain-of-sale clauses can seriously disadvantage your offer. If you must include one, limit it to 30 or 60 days, if possible.

- **Disclosures**. State law varies on the type of disclosures a seller is required to make, but your offer should include a timeframe for making them and an opt-out if serious issues are revealed.

New York Note: Condo or co-op board approval is usually an assumed contingency, but sometimes it is included in the contract. That is, if the building's condo or co-op board won't accept you as an owner, the deal is void.

WHEN TO ASK FOR CONCESSIONS

Concessions can work both ways—some advantage the seller and others advantage the buyer. For example, asking for help with closing costs benefits the buyer, while offering leaseback or a flexible move-in date may benefit sellers who aren't ready to move as of the closing date.

Closing cost concessions get tricky if you're financing your home with a conventional loan: concede too much and your lender will reduce your mortgage amount, negating the whole point of the concession. The following are current guidelines for conforming loans for a primary or secondary home:

Loan-to-Value	Amount Allowed
Greater than 90%	3%
75% to 90%	6%
Less than 75%	9%

For government-backed loans, the limits are different. FHA loans limit concessions to buyers' points only—anything over that amount has to be made up in the down payment. VA loans limit concessions to 4%.

If you are buying the home to use as a rental property, you can only get 2% in closing cost concessions on conventional loans, regardless of the loan-to-value amount.

Appliances are another concession you may want to consider in your offer. Although the range and oven almost always stay with the home, you may want to ask for other appliances such as the refrigerator, washer, and dryer. If there is any other personal property you want, be sure to specify it in the offer.

If you're buying new construction, you can ask for concessions in the form of upgrades or customization. If you're buying a condo, the developer may concede a free storage unit or parking space, for example.

AFTER THE OFFER: WHAT TO EXPECT

Once you've written a purchase offer with your agent, he or she will present it to the listing agent and one of three things will happen. The seller will: 1) accept the offer as is; 2) reject it outright; or 3) make a counteroffer.

Rejected

If the offer is rejected, this usually means that the seller has either already accepted another offer on the home or decided that the gap between what they want and your offer is so wide that there's no point in opening negotiations. If your offer is rejected, it's usually best to move on to the next property you're interested in.

Can you submit another offer to the same seller? Technically, yes, but there's probably no good reason to do so. If the seller is already in negotiations with another buyer, he can't negotiate with you. If it's rejected for some other reason, the seller may not be particularly motivated at this time.

If you do decide to submit another offer, be direct and put your absolute best offer on the table. And then walk away if the seller responds with anything other than acceptance.

Countered

If the seller responds with a counteroffer, you're still in the game. You can either accept the counteroffer within the time specified, or reply with your own counteroffer. During the negotiation phase, you're both trying to reach a price on the property that satisfies everyone. This is where concessions come in, for both the buyer and the seller.

This process of back-and-forth negotiation can last for several hours—or several days. Ultimately, you'll either wind up with a purchase agreement, or you'll start the process all over again on a new property.

Accepted

Once the offer is accepted, and both parties have signed the purchase contract, it's legally binding. In other words, if you back out of the deal for any reason not covered in the contract, you forfeit your earnest money. If the seller backs out, you could potentially sue for breach of contract.

New York Note: In NY, the process of negotiating a final purchase contract generally falls to the attorneys. Once your attorney and the seller's attorney have reached agreement, you'll sign the contract and your attorney will forward it to the seller, along with your earnest money.

POST-CONTRACT AND INSPECTIONS

Now things start to move quickly. Your lender schedules the appraisal and prepares your loan package for underwriting. You, your agent, and your attorney start the process of satisfying all of the contingencies, securing title insurance, and preparing closing paperwork. Your main job at this point is to respond to any requests documents from your lender or attorney and make sure your money is ready for closing. Don't make any big purchases, open any new credit accounts, or change jobs during this time, as you could jeopardize your home loan.

> **New York Note:** The condo/co-op board application can be as much work as your mortgage application. If an interview is required, it may take time to coordinate your schedule with board members. Sometimes they only interview once per month, and if you miss the interview day, you've added another month's delay to the closing process.

You may also need to negotiate around the contingencies, especially the home inspection. Depending on what the contract says, and what the inspection turns up, you have four options if the home doesn't pass with flying colors:

- **You can cancel the purchase agreement outright.** You get your earnest money back and you're free to make an offer on another home. This may be the best option if the issues are structurally significant or extremely costly to repair.
- **You can renegotiate the price.** Under this option, you get to supervise any actual repairs yourself, using your contractors, after the sale is complete. This may be appealing if the new price is favorable and you actually have enough cash available to do the work. It's also an appealing option for sellers, since they don't have the headache of making repairs.

- **You can ask the seller to do repairs**. If you go this route, you need to be precise about what you want done, when the work needs to be finished, what inspections are required, and any documentation that should be provided by the seller.

- **You can do nothing.** If the issues are minor and common to "used" homes, it may be to your advantage not to hold up the purchase while the owner fixes every defect. This is especially true if you bought the home at a discounted price—a long list of minor repairs in a contract amendment could unnecessarily antagonize the seller and cause the deal to fall apart.

Once all the negotiations are complete, the contingencies satisfied, the loan approved, and the final walk-through complete, you're ready to close.

KEY TAKEAWAYS:

- Comparables and other financial data are important when you're deciding what to offer on a home, but don't forget to factor in how badly you want the property. If you'll really regret not getting this house, make an attractive offer.

- Show you're serious about your offer by putting down a sizeable earnest money deposit.

- Both buyers and sellers can use concessions to move negotiations along and close a deal.

CHAPTER 9.
CLOSING ON YOUR
FIRST HOME

You'd be forgiven for thinking the hard part's over, now that the contract is signed and your financing is well underway. The truth is, you're not sprinting to the finish line...you're starting the last leg of the marathon.

The "average" time to close is around 45 days, but statistics from the National Association of REALTORS suggest that about a third of all home closings have at least one delay. Most of the time, it's a snag with financing (please, no new credit accounts or job changes!), but other things can hold you up too. However, if you've gotten through the appraisal and inspections process, you're probably in pretty good shape.

Here's what you can expect the process to look like when you're closing on your first home.

STEPS TO CLOSING

Although these steps won't look exactly the same for everyone, and the timeline to complete each one may be a bit different, these are the basic processes that need to be completed before you can sign your last document, hand over your cash, and get the keys to your new home.

Clearing the contingencies

All purchase contracts have contingencies built into them, covering things like the appraisal, home inspections, condo or co-op board approval, and financing approval. Before you can head to the closing table, you'll need to negotiate a resolution to any contingencies.

For example, if the appraisal is low, you may need to split the difference with the seller in cash. Or, if the inspection turns up something worrisome, you may need to bargain over a repair addendum.

Your real estate agent will work with you to make sure the co-op or condo board approval process goes well. He or she will advise you on the financial requirements and any additional documentation you may need for proof of funds. If you've chosen your team well, your agent already knows whether or not your financials work for the building you've picked, so approval should be a formality at this point.

Obtaining title insurance

In order to close on your loan, your lender requires title insurance, which protects the lender from any claims or disputes against the property. Before the title company will issue a policy, a title search must be performed to establish three things:

- That the seller has the right to sell the property and is acting in good faith

- Whether there are any easements or use restrictions with the property
- Whether there are any liens, assessments, or other claims against the property

If the title is "clear," the title company will issue a lender's title insurance policy. It's a good idea to get an owner's title insurance policy as well to protect you from any future claims. The buyer always pays for the lender's policy, and for the owner's policy as well in most states. In some states, the seller pays for the owner's policy.

Passing the lender's underwriting

Underwriting is the bank's process of ensuring your loan package meets the lender's risk profile. It's generally a four-part process that involves:

- **Analyzing your credit report.** If you have any late payments or collection accounts, even old ones, you'll probably need to provide additional documentation.
- **Verifying the income and employment information** you provided on your loan application. You'll usually need to provide two years' worth of tax returns and W-2s. In some cases, the lender may confirm your information by calling your employer.
- **Examining the appraisal.** The underwriter will make sure the appraiser followed the lender's guidelines and adjustments, and that the loan

amount falls within acceptable loan-to-value ratios for the mortgage you applied for.

- **Confirming your assets**. The lender is scrutinizing your down payment to make sure it came from your own funds. If a relative gifted you down payment money, you'll need documentation for that. Also, be sure the money is sitting in your account for at least three statement cycles before applying for your mortgage. Most lenders want to see that the money is in your account for at least two months prior to closing. They'll also make sure you have adequate cash reserves after your down payment and closing costs are paid. Some lenders require one month's mortgage payment, while others may ask for up to six months or more. Be prepared to provide statements from your checking, savings, and investment accounts.

Most lenders use an automated underwriting system in combination with a human underwriter who completes the deci   loan officer or attorney is the   he underwriter. Be sure to resp   nt or information requests so th   d.

Reviewing the closing disclosure or settlement statement

Lenders must send you a good faith estimate of closing costs within three days of receiving your loan application. Three days before your scheduled closing date, your lender must send you the closing disclosure. This document shows your *actual* closing costs—the amount of money you need to have, often in certified funds, at closing.

You'll want to go over these documents carefully to make sure there are no significant changes. Ask your attorney or lender to explain anything you don't understand. Double-check the terms of the mortgage, especially the interest rate and payment amount.

Completing the walk-through

Your agent will schedule the final walk-through, usually for within 24 hours of closing. During this time, the home should be empty except for any personal property included in the purchase contract (unless you've agreed to a leaseback after closing).

This is your chance to make sure the home is in the condition agreed upon when the offer was made, and that all the appliances, fixtures, faucets, windows, doors, and HVAC units (and anything else you can think to check) are working properly. Don't feel rushed during this process—and bring up any issues immediately with your agent.

Compiling your documents and cash

Your attorney or settlement agent will let you know exactly how much money you'll need to bring and in what form you need to bring it. In some cases, you may need certified funds, and in others, a personal check will do. And of course, you'll need to bring a government-issued ID that matches the name on the loan and the title.

You may also need to bring proof of homeowners insurance, any inspection reports, or additional documents your lender requested to approve the loan.

WHAT TO EXPECT ON CLOSING DAY

Closing day is a paperwork-fest: in some states, buyers sign close to 100 documents. Be sure to stretch your signing hand!

Depending on where you live, your closing could be attended by several different people: you (and your homebuying partner, if you have one), the escrow agent, the closing agent, your attorney, the title agent, the lender's representative, the real estate agents, the seller, and the seller's attorney.

Keep in mind, it's not always a big crowd. In some states, the attorney is also the closing agent, or the escrow agent acts as closing agent. If the seller pre-signed his transfer and title documents, he may choose not to attend.

Closing usually takes between one and two hours, but don't feel rushed. Ask questions about anything you don't understand, and don't sign until you're comfortable with the answer.

Although the documentation and closing process might seem complex, the purpose of closing, or settlement, is fairly straightforward: to transfer ownership from the seller to you, to register the new deed in your name, and to exchange and distribute funds.

EVERYTHING YOU EVER WANTED TO KNOW ABOUT CLOSING COSTS

Closing costs vary greatly—by where you live, the type of property you buy, the financial institution handling the loan, and the type of loan you choose. Let's start by defining some of the terms you might see on your closing paperwork.

Keep in mind that this is an exhaustive list, and your loan likely won't have all of these costs.

- **Application fee**. Not all lenders charge an application fee, but it usually includes things like a credit report, appraisal fee, and loan processing fees. It's generally negotiable if you ask.
- **Appraisal fee**. This fee goes to the licensed professional hired by the lender to appraise your home.
- **Attorney fees**. This could cover fees for your real estate attorney, the closing attorney, the co-op attorney, and/or the lender's attorney.
- **Board application fee**. The fee paid to your condo or co-op board to process your application.
- **Credit report**. Your lender will pull credit reports, as will the condo or co-op board if you go that route.
- **Document fees**. This covers preparing the documents themselves, as well as any necessary courier services to keep closing on schedule.
- **Escrow deposit**. Lenders typically expect two months' worth of property taxes and mortgage insurance to be deposited into an escrow account.

- **Escrow fees**. This is paid to the title company, escrow agent, or attorney actually handling the closing.

- **Escrow for common charges**. If you buy a condo, you may need to put money in an escrow account to cover common charges.

- **Escrow for maintenance**. If you buy a co-op, you usually need to put at least two months' worth of maintenance fees in an escrow account.

- **Filing fees**. Administrative charges for filing any required documents with appropriate city or county agencies.

- **FHA UFMIP** (Upfront Mortgage Insurance Premium). FHA loans require 1.75% of the loan amount as an upfront payment for mortgage insurance.

- **Hazard insurance**. If you live in certain areas prone to certain natural disasters such as tornados or floods, your lender may require supplemental hazard insurance in addition to a standard homeowners policy.

- **HOA transfer fees**. The seller generally pays for this document, which shows that fees are current, and includes a copy of the HOA's financials and minutes.

- **Home inspection**. These are fees paid to the companies conducting any home inspections ordered on the property.

- **Homeowners insurance**. Typically the lender requires that the first year's premium be put in escrow.

- **Lender's title insurance**. The cost for the policy is always listed as a separate line item from the title search itself.
- **Loan discount points**. This is the prepaid interest that buys down the interest rate on your loan.
- **Mansion tax**. In some locations, there is an extra surcharge on high-value properties. In NYC, for example, the tax applies to home sales at $1 million or more.
- **Move-in fees**. Many buildings charge a fee to move in, which may include an elevator deposit.
- **Notary fee**. Certain documents may need to be notarized. This may be a separate line item on the settlement statement.
- **Origination fee**. Covers administrative fees and is typically 1% of the loan amount. Many times this single fee replaces many of the smaller document and credit report fees.
- **Owner's title insurance**. This is optional, and may be paid by either the buyer or the seller, depending on where you live.
- **Prepaid interest**. Most lenders charge you the amount of interest on your loan between the date of closing and the date your first mortgage payment is due.
- **Private mortgage insurance** (PMI). If you put less than 20% down, you'll have to pay PMI. Your lender usually requires the first month's premium at closing.
- **Recording fees**. This fee is paid to city or county government for recording the property records.

- **Stamp tax**. This is a tax levied on certain financial transactions involved in buying a home.
- **Survey fee**. Some states require that all property lines are verified prior to closing.
- **Title search**. This covers costs associated with verifying a clear title prior to issuing title insurance.
- **Transfer tax**. Some areas charge a tax for transferring property titles.
- **Underwriting fee**. This covers the costs associated with verifying and approving your loan application.
- **Wire transfer fee**. If your attorney or escrow agent wires any funds on your behalf, you will pay a fee for the service.

Nationwide, the average cost for buyers to close on a house is between 2% and 4% of the purchase price of the home, although costs will be significantly higher in some areas.

Many closing costs are negotiable, especially the broadly generic ones like "application fees," "origination fees," and "document fees." Considering these could add up to thousands of dollars, it pays to mortgage-shop and get specific information about how the lender calculates their internal administrative fees to process and close your loan.

CONDO VERSUS CO-OP CLOSING COSTS

The difference in closing costs for a condo versus a co-op is fairly significant. When you buy a condo, you are actually buying a piece of real property: you own your unit and a percentage of the common areas. With a co-op, however, you are buying shares in a corporation that is your building. Condos are considered real property, while co-ops are considered personal property.

Here's what the fee difference between a condo and co-op looks like on a $1 million apartment in New York, assuming a 20% down payment and $800,000 mortgage:

	Condo	Co-op
Attorney Fees	$3,000	$3,000
NYC Mansion Tax	$10,000	$10,000
Title Insurance	$6,000	$0*
Bank Attorney	$1,500	$1,500
Mortgage Recording Tax	$15,400	$0
Miscellaneous Closing Costs	$4,000	$4,000
Total	**$39,900**	**$18,500**

*Lately, the trend is to obtain title insurance on co-ops. You may or may not have this expense if you go the co-op route.

New York Note: Most co-ops and even some condos charge a "flip tax," which is technically not a tax, but a fee charged on the sale or transfer of an apartment to generate revenue for the building. If your building charges this fee, it will be documented in the by-laws. This fee is in addition to any other transfer taxes paid to the city or state at closing.

The flip tax can be assessed in many different ways, such as a percentage of sales price (typically 1 to 3 percent), a flat fee, a percentage of the seller's profits, or a dollar amount per share in the co-op. Although it's usually paid by the seller, all fees are negotiable in an NYC real estate transaction. Your lawyer will do due diligence prior to closing and negotiate any flip tax payments on your behalf.

CLOSING COSTS THAT MAY BE TAX-DEDUCTIBLE

While this section isn't intended to substitute for the advice of a tax accountant or attorney, there are some costs that may be deductible in the year you bought your home if you itemize your taxes:

- Sales and real estate taxes charged to you at closing or paid by your lender
- Mortgage interest paid at closing
- Loan origination points (only on a primary residence and only in certain situations—ask a tax professional)

The rules about what *can't* be deducted are a bit more clear. In most cases, **none of the following closing costs** can be deducted at tax time:

- Insurance, including homeowners, fire, flood, or title
- Title fees
- Attorney fees
- Appraisal and inspection fees
- Transfer taxes

KEY TAKEAWAYS:

- Most homes close in about six weeks, although one in three is delayed by financing or other issues.
- Buyer closing costs are generally between 2% and 4% of the purchase price of the home, but in some areas, they can be significantly higher.
- Co-ops are considered personal property, not real property, so closing costs for co-ops are much lower than for those of condos.

NEXT STEPS

You should now feel ready to confidently start your homebuying journey.

Remember, this guide is not meant to replace the personalized advice of a good team of real estate professionals.

If you need help choosing the right agent or attorney, you're more than welcome to contact me at homebuyer@anthonyspark.com or 212-401-2990. I'll be happy to point you in the right direction.

GLOSSARY

MORTGAGE LOAN TERMS TO KNOW

Amortization—The loan repayment schedule showing the portion of the payment applied to principal and interest each month.

Appraisal—An estimate of your home's value provided by a professional appraiser. It includes physically inspecting the home and comparing it to similar homes that have sold in the area.

Debt-to-income ratio (DTI)—The total of your monthly debt payments divided by your gross monthly income, expressed as a percentage. Most lenders require a DTI of 36% or below to qualify for a mortgage loan.

Equity—The difference between what your home is worth and the balance on any loans against it. If your home is worth $600,000 and you have $400,000 in loans, you have $200,000 in home equity.

Escrow—This is an account maintained by your lender and used to pay property taxes and insurance payments on your home. A portion of your monthly mortgage payment is held in escrow to cover these costs.

Good faith estimate—An estimate of your closing costs prepared by your lender.

Homeowners insurance—Coverage that provides financial protection for your home. You need homeowners coverage before you can close on your mortgage. It must name the lender as the payee in the event the home is destroyed.

Loan-to-value ratio (LTV)—This figure is determined by dividing the mortgage amount against the appraised value of the home. You generally need an LTV of 80% to qualify for a conventional mortgage.

Origination fee—This is what your lender charges you for making a loan. It can include application fees, appraisal fees, underwriting fees, and document fees. Be sure to ask what's included in fees with nonspecific names like "origination" or "processing" or "funding" fees.

PITI—Most mortgage payments include PITI, or principal, interest, taxes, and insurance. The principal and interest portions are paid to the lender, and the lender holds your taxes and insurance in escrow to pay those bills on your behalf.

Points—Generally used to buy down your mortgage interest rate, points are fees equal to 1% of the loan amount. Also called "discount points."

PMI (primary or private mortgage insurance)—If you get a mortgage loan with an LTV of more than 80%, you'll have to buy PMI to protect your lender in case you default. PMI generally costs between 0.5% and 1.0% of the loan amount each year.

Title insurance—Lenders require buyers to get title insurance to make sure that the property is free and clear of any liens or other claims before they issue a mortgage. This is part of your mortgage closing costs.

Underwriting—The formal process of financial verification and analysis a lender uses to determine the level of risk involved in making a loan. In most cases, it involves credit score, repayment capacity, and collateral. The underwriter usually has the final say in approving the loan.

ABOUT THE AUTHOR

Anthony S. Park is host of the popular podcast *Simple Money Wins* (available on iTunes, Google Play, and anthonyspark.com).

He is a New York executor, attorney, and entrepreneur. Anthony's cases have been featured in many places, including the *Wall Street Journal*, *New York Times*, CNBC, and *MarketWatch*.

INDEX

Made in the USA
Las Vegas, NV
03 January 2022

40179181R00075